Borrowed Light

)(°)(°)(

Ken Haas

Grateful acknowledgment is made to the following journals and anthologies in which some of these poems first appeared:

Alabama Literary Review, "Atlantic City, 1959"; *Burningword*, "The Choices They Made," "Everything"; *Catamaran*, "At Mile Rocks"; *The Coachella Review*, "Sleeping in the Crack"; *Descant*, "The Path of Totality"; *Existere*, "Tea"; *Faultline*, "Milpitas Sunset," "Xiu-Xiu"; *Hawai'i Pacific Review*, "Waking at Night in Kailua"; *The Healing Muse*, "The Colonoscopai"; *The Hiram Poetry Review*, "Unidentified Objects"; *Lullwater Review*, "Trane"; *The MacGuffin*, "War"; *Menacing Hedge*, "Private Sky"; *Mudlark*, "The Alternate Merge"; *Moon City Review*, "God's Widow"; *Natural Bridge*, "Gin and Tonic"; *Nimrod*, "The Sound a Key Makes"; *pamplemousse*, "On Being Slapped By a Woman I Don't Know," "Bad Homburg"; *Poet Lore*, "Lottery Day, 1970"; *Prism*, "The Rusted Horse"; *Quiddity*, "Eyebrows"; *Red Wheelbarrow*, "Truxel Road"; *The Schuylkill Valley Journal*, "OLQM"; *Squaw Valley Review*, "Borrowed Light," "The Clone"; *Stickman Review*, "Madame Butterfly"; *Streetlight*, "Speaking in Tongues"; *Studio One*, "Learning to Kayak"; *Tattoo Highway*, "Birdsong"; *Word Fountain*, "Perfection"

Anthologies
The Place that Inhabits Us, "Land's End," Sixteen Rivers Press, 2010; *Ecopoetry of California, Fire and Rain*, "Otter," Scarlett Tanager Books, 2018

ISBN 978-1-7326501-9-0
Printed in the United States of America

RED MOUNTAIN PRESS
Seattle, Washington
www.redmountainpress.us

for Edith and Edgar

BIRDSONG

Regarding the question of nature or nurture,
we quarantined some birds at birth,
finches mostly, to see what songs
they might come to know,

whether they would sing at all.
Their brethren in the wild meanwhile
were learning many tribal hymns
for waking and working, loving and mourning.

When the culled were returned to the fold
they did have songs, only a few
of kettle and clock,
cloistered heart and challenged soul.

They were welcomed nonetheless
and taught the standards by and by
as their own songs vanished
in the mallow and cottonwood trees.

But at the moment of return
when the whole flock was gathered
frightened and still:
what strangeness, what stories.

SLEEPING IN THE CRACK

For a time in first grade
I had what they then called school refusal.
Mostly because Mrs. Karasick
locked me in the chalk closet for two hours
over a point about French Impressionism
that I had disputed.

My father made up a song for me to sing
on the way to P.S. 152 which started
Heigh-ho, heigh-ho, it's off to school we go....
We practiced it every evening in the mirror
until I could see that I was smiling.
And I sang it, leaving home.

At night sometimes I woke to what were surely
Soviet airplanes buzzing the Bronx
and sought safety in my parents' room.
They had separate double beds
joined by two large steel clips
hooked to the hardwood frames,
separate sheets but a single blanket
so they had something to bicker about
even while unconscious.

They were dangerous in different ways
so I burrowed under the blanket,
wedged myself into the one-inch doorway
between the beds, and slept.

Years later someone told me
that the adult I had become
could return and rescue that boy,
be what he needed.

But even back then I had Simo's pizza,
a Moose Skowron glove,
Janie Siegel next door,

who told me there were kids
with nowhere. Not even a crack.
And no song to sing.

OLQM

Not one of the lapsed Catholics I fell for later
could guess what those letters stood for.
Most knew "Our Lady," a few got "Queen,"
but the "M" escaped even the most canonical.
"Mother," they might say, "Miracles" or "Mercy,"
just not the true punch line to an orange code stitched
in the lime-green ties of the schoolboys on Arden Street
and in their sisters' plaid wool skirts hemmed below the knees,
knees that nonetheless saw daylight furled on the A train,
saw us public school spuds dazed
by their doughy blush and the rumbling heat,
knees that, like all long-clenched things,
might go anywhere from there, and with anyone.
So praise the boys and girls with the monograms,
praise their fathers who believed in labor and country
and that college was for the Jews,
praise their mothers slipping through the back door
of the Kosher butcher for the lean corned beef,
praise Joe Duffy reading Joyce on the ballyard stoop
and Kevin Simmons with his parboiled face
carving a hooked cross in the library door,
praise the land those boys flew off to
and the red-bandanaed men who killed them both,
praise the jade torrents of the Mekong Delta
and the emerald mists of the Celtic Sea,
the olive body bags, mossy unmarked graves,
orange hair and flaming hair,
praise, too, Maggie Conlon
who crossed herself before she crossed the line,
praise all who've had faith
and those who've had enough of it,
praise Our Lady Queen of Martyrs.

TRANE

None of us in 1966 wanted to be a white kid
from the Bronx. So I rode the subway down
to hear the man who might make me cool.

The gasbags claimed he played higher math.
His friends said he practiced like a guy with no talent.
This cat who told Miles that once he got started
he didn't know how to stop. Yet could start
anywhere, like with raindrops on roses,
drive past the ghost town of pride,
then bring you back safe,
to some other home.

Such a sweet tooth that his horn was often
clogged with sugar; such a soft touch
that he packed binoculars to look for stars
where you couldn't even find the moon.
A navy man, like my dad.
Saint of a church in the city where I moved to live.

That night at the Vanguard he blew in tongues.
Two hours straight. One song.
Ended on his knees. Dropped a stitch
I can still pick up or use for grip
in any ditch, on any ledge.

He emptied his arms in a wave that even now
          speaks to the kind of man I could become,
          teaches what a gift is,
          warns there's little sing-along,
                    what just happened
                    just happened
                    and what comes next doesn't follow,
          asks if I'm in this
or just listening.

LOTTERY DAY, 1970

We're taking infield practice and shagging flies,
Jersey heat dripping from the bills of our caps,
"Black Magic Woman" on a distant transistor,
kids splashing and shouting in the public pool.
The ribbing and the girl talk are on low.
Someone hits a ball into the tennis courts.
A man in white shorts throws it back gently.
Today the war is coming home.

In an hour my mother will meet me at the door,
still in her nightgown, having watched TV all day
as blue plastic capsules
were drawn from two separate drums,
one of which was full of birthdays.
A Winston in her hand, her eyes will be red,
but she'll be smiling.
All she will say is, "316."

I backhand a grounder near second.
The shortstop turns two.
Crickets are out at noon.
We're all friends—we're all nineteen—
our moms at home,
glued to flickering screens,
while we're out playing the game we know.

Waking at Night in Kailua

I have come to a place
        where dark, backlit shapes
beat madly behind the braided bamboo shade,
broad, brooding shapes that may or may not be
the cut, swaying leaves of coconut palm,
the spiked beaks of Heliconia or frigate,
        where I can't distinguish
rain wash from wind rush
        and feel what I can't see,
whirling breath of a teakwood ceiling fan,
cool, pulling back, coming again,
        where in nightly dreams the doors
have been torn from my house back home,
lizards crisscross the walls, turtles snap in the tubs,
friends want me gone,
they're tired of my anger,
        I have come half-asleep,
from north or south,
outside in or inside out,
        I sit up, run to the breakers, dive
not praying for sun-up,
and tip the wave crests with any dim light I have
or just meet darkness with darkness.

ATLANTIC CITY, 1959

Sunburn and saltwater taffy,
butterscotch fudge sliced thin and often,
young bodies coddled in mounds of sand.

A mustachioed sailor in spandex skivvies
boxes a kangaroo, the new Miss America
waves by in a top-down Eldorado
and a waitress dives headlong on horseback
toward a pool at the end of the pier.

At dusk the wives are off to the club
in summer dresses to hear Frank and Sammy,
husbands flipping the last of a Chesterfield
over the rail, or beading up in booths
on late calls to lovers in Brooklyn,
when here and there the lines go down,
their coins and many more that night
hung in the dead machines.

Under the boardwalk my immigrant dad
is unplugging the phones.
We will be back near dawn, father below,
re-connecting the wires of holiday
to the sockets of need,
son above, silver quarters and dimes
rushing to his pockets like sea foam.

I'm Spartacus

Fifteen years after liberation of the camps
we understood in the concrete playgrounds of the Bronx why
the leader of the Roman slave revolt in the Oscar-winning movie
could not be played by Izzy Demsky, just as the role
of Antoninus, who first stood to claim his captain's name,
so none of them would die alone,
could not be played by Bernie Schwartz,
just as Emanuel Goldenberg could not be Little Caesar
or Hyman Greenblatt be Ben Cartwright, or
Jacob Garfinkle light a serious fire in Lana Turner.

But we did not understand, really,
ashamed to speak their new, their Hollywood names.
After all, their neighbors were not being rounded up.
They could have fed the kids some other way.

And word always gets out.
Their stage names are listed next to their birth names now
in a section called "verbal nose jobs" on a white pride website
suddenly meticulous about the facts.
A nose by any other name.

And for us a new understanding, from the diaspora,
lawyers, brokers, artists and shrinks without a clue
where our names came from or how.
Spartacus took the name of his homeland's cultured conquerors.
So tell me which is the flag of a warrior,
which the mark of a traitor or a fool.
Shame is a worm that turns.
Too late now to stand in the schoolyard and shout
to its echoing walls, "I'm Greenblatt
and Greene, Garfinkle and Garfield,
Douglas and Demsky, Curtis and Schwartz."

THE ALTERNATE MERGE

is what separates us from the beasts
            cracks the cabbie in Jersey
as we grind like chipped gear teeth
            toward the steel cervix
of the George Washington Bridge.

            He waves in a puce-haired coed
with labret, who crosses herself
            after flipping him off,
then noses out a flouncing Lincoln
            with smoke greasing every seam,
lets "Life's a bitch and so am I" slip past
            on the bumper of a Teaneck housewife,
cuts no slack for the Civic
            whose dashboard saint's
getting its ears boxed by pink foam dice.

            All interleaved with his own jagged rant:
He's still pissed about the way Big Pussy died,
            caught his wife last May
snorting coke off some stockbroker's belly,
            his youngest has migraines,
a broken nose and a gun, he likes
            this one's breasts and that one's hat,
says don't the sun's billion H-bombs
            make a heaven here on earth.

But that's it. Not one more let in.
            Last justice doled as the toll gets paid.
Then we're all in a line above Hudson's river,
            the Mohawk and Hoosic still in its blood,
the saw-toothed spires still at its side,
            the old oyster island,
where throngs fed the dream to gagging,
            still on the tip of its tongue.

GIN AND TONIC

To control malaria in colonial India
they washed the quinine down with soda water
which was still quite bitter, in fact glowed in the dark.
Until a bright lance sergeant with tea-colored pith helmet
started adding liquor, ice and a thin wheel of lime.
Not just any liquor, but spirits that reminded him of home,
pressed dry from white grain and juniper berries
with names like Gordon's, Beefeater, Plymouth.
He couldn't have known about
the boys down at Vinny's telling jokes till the ball game ends,
the single mom on her vinyl divan after the kids are asleep,
the software salesman at Logan waiting out a snowstorm.
He hadn't invented civilization,
just knew it's a drink you have to keep civilizing,
forever swizzling the familiar back into the foreign
until you can taste, perhaps even see
what you will never have again.

PERFECTION

In junior high Spanish class
Mr. Koochman handed out nicknames
that followed us into the streets.

The pouty ingénue was Labios Levine,
the over-developed blonde Melones Morgan,
the kid from the projects Kong Coleman.
The hairy one became Oso,
the sweaty one Puerco,
and the frail, nervous one
who rode the D train early
with the night nurses and winos,
was dubbed Hércules.

This was the Bronx in 1965.

Koochman, a cadaver in tweed,
gave a daily quiz, and as of March
Hércules hadn't missed a question.
So the tests got harder.
And the subway became a study hall
for the boy's now-epic obsession.
Until, with two weeks left in the school year,
Koochman, understanding he was beaten,
called Hércules to stand before him
and, quivering, yelled, "You are a machine,"
in his pustuled face. The kid just turned
toward the empty blackboard,
slid a piece of chalk from its metal ledge,
and wrote down his name.

At our fortieth reunion a woman resembling Melones
ran up to me, shouting, "Hércules, Hércules…"
She had apparently placed second in the class
then spent her career as a Spanish translator,

so was devastated to learn that I
had not become the U.S. Ambassador to Spain.
I was about to tell her she had the wrong guy—
that was another boy.
Then I remembered who we all were once.

LEARNING TO KAYAK

Like the Nunivak boy, stitched
roll-tight by a proud mother
into the cockpit of his hunting bark,
all sealskin and whalebone,
I am told that
          before I can brace the swells
which have come a thousand miles to meet me,
          before I can even launch or land,
          I must learn to idle
in what Inuit elders called the soup,
the liquid wilderness
brewed by the shore and its nearest wave,
last to feel the earth and give up shape.

Bow pointed fiercely into the break line,
          I must find the fluid switch
between headlong plow into the final spill
and full-out backstroke against the undertow,
          make short work of comings and goings,
until my body and its body are drunk
with the ways of swash and backwash,
          after long days of trial
          hardly paddling at all.

Here is the furious lull,
the simmering meal,
the endlessly rocking means to all ends,
where the current is lost
and the moon has let go of the tide.
          The ocean at samba,
          the surf's foam baton.
Let me stay here as long as I can.

II

SANCTUARY

My grandfather thought he was a German,
dashing in his Pickelhaube, iron cross
and bullet from Verdun, until they told him,
"No, you are not one of us,"
and a clothier named Stern in North Dakota,
who didn't know him, signed some papers,
which sailed him elsewhere, so twenty years later
he could watch *The Hunchback of Notre Dame*
with me on a black and white box in the Bronx.
Quasimodo was an ugly wreck. I remember
the gap tooth, pig nose and seesaw eyes.
The townsfolk teased and menaced him.
My grandfather said, "He is one of us."
Esmeralda was Maureen O'Hara,
who had curls, breasts and a tambourine
that could make a boy forget he was six.
Hounded as a gypsy, she was set to be hanged.
My grandfather said, "She is one of us."
I asked, "But how do I know?"
And he said the same way Stern knew
two half-continents and an ocean away,
without a speck of ash on the hood of his car.
At which precise moment the hunchback
swung down on a rope to scoop up the gypsy,
fly her to the belfry and shout, over and over,
a solitary word,
in a splendid voice that belied his brokenness.
It's not often that you know exactly
what a word means the first time you hear it.
Or that every time you hear it after
someone nothing like you
is sailing for your shore.

BAD HOMBURG

Roman legions took the waters there.
Count Friedrich built a fountain for his English bride.
Kaiser Wilhelm, after gobbling states piecemeal
then spitting Deutschland out whole,
drank iron from the native springs whose magic
still steams past Goethe's white tower
into the light ether of baroque façades, oompah bands
and the foothills of the Taunus mountains.

The only thing my father ever mentioned
about his home town
was the summer day he leaned so long against
the limestone fence circling the famed fountain
that his knee swelled, got wedged
and the piqued burgermeisters,
after soberly debating all options,
in the presence of half the town come out to watch,
chiseled crescents in the cherished rails
and set the boy free.

Not long after he passed,
a few childhood friends gathered for schnapps
somewhere in South Florida
with thick air, scant history and no cures.
Hannah Stein recalled Klaus Heidrich barking
that her nose looked like the number six.
Max Rosen spoke of his grandma
rapping him with her offended cane
as he hummed a march song heard in the streets.
Fritz Levy said he'd gone back in spring
and the fountain fence was still carved out,
could not be mended, though they'd tried,
said he asked the townsfolk how it got that way,
but no one seemed to know,
though they knew about the Romans, the Kaiser
and the princess bride.

WAR

When the archivist at Ellis Island met my father
a few years before his death and asked
what was the most memorable time of his life,
he said it was the War but wouldn't embellish.

And when he got sick, the family gathered, waiting
for the aneurysm to burst, with hospice nurses
in eight-hour shifts to catheterize him,
give him shots of hydromorphone for the pain.
They were professionally attentive, sidetracked
only once in a while by a magazine, a cell phone,
the food Mom couldn't stop cooking.

Except for nurse Carlos, back two years
from a tour in Iraq, who never for a second
took his eyes off Dad, soaked up his accounts
of Okinawa, sat with him in the bathroom,
watched him gaze out the window,
eased the coffee cup from his hand
when he dozed in his chair.
Nurse Carlos—a rock from East Newark,
buzz-cut, laconic, *Keep Watch*
burned in black on his neck.
Dad—his tired tales and the soul we doubted,
laced with the prayers of the battlefield dead.

So it was surely as the old Seabee had dreamed
a thousand times: After he went in for a nap,
Carlos in tow, the rest of us joking, reminiscing,
making plans in the living room,
a soldier was the last one to see him alive.

THE CHOICES THEY MADE

During Geraldine Ferraro's run for vice president
as a congresswoman from Queens in 1984,
one burly heckler on the campaign trail
questioned how Archie Bunker
had ever elected her,
to which she replied, "He didn't; Edith did."
Which happened to be my mother's name,
and when Edith Baines Bunker
took side stage in the top sitcom of the seventies,
Edith Klein Haas sat right beside her,
making it easy for us to notice what they didn't do:
object or judge, burst balloons,
say *this is what I want*,
say *no* to their outrageous men,
hide the racing form from their fathers,
or ever miss *Days of Our Lives*. Instead
they wore their brassieres, practiced being
unembarrassed, learned to type, played canasta,
and boiled the parts of meat that could be eaten
no other way. And they understood
the black neighbors, the lesbian cousin, understood
that their hairsprayed heads would not be pictured
on the book jacket for *The Greatest Generation*.
Their superpower was not invisibility,
but optimism; Fred and Ginger twirling in air,
that cigarette ash on top of the scrambled eggs
always pretending to be a cherry.
Long before all of which, the sailor my mother
had met in an ice cream parlor prewar
came back dirty, darkened, craving a son.
And although the odds clearly favored delivery
of another just like him—man with two separate hearts,
one to love and one to deny—
when he insisted she don his favorite nightgown,
the chiffon of lace yoke and floral appliqué,
Edith did.

THE SOUND A KEY MAKES

When it's your father
and he's brought cannoli or a game
in which blue Whirlaway
races green Seabiscuit
across the linoleum world.

When it's your father
and the look in your mother's eye
says *it will be the strap this time*
and your heart will dig its own grave.

When it's your wife,
whose spiral kisses on your back
speak to the unspoken,
whose eyes never look away.

When it's your own hand,
hoping she isn't home
and, now, she's not.

Each click,
brass voicing brass, as different
as the room in which it rings—
one where the door's unopened,
another where it's shut;
one where the keyhole beckons,
one where it tells the truth.

THE RUSTED HORSE

for my father

Not molded, but soldered and welded,
he points away from the cabins and cars
toward the trail-less, chaparral hills.
Strips have been cut from his sheet metal frame.
Light and shadow take turns at his core.
Flies doze on his chestnut haunches.
Through and around him, a breeze
flicks up dust and combs back the bunchgrass.
Sometimes his ribboned mane ripples
and glints like fool's gold in the valley sun.
Wherever you are now, is there time to linger?
Can you hear jays hollering in the maple,
dragonflies humming the moss-bound pond?
I imagine you're still not of the landscape
you inhabit, though the parts of it most themselves
have taken you in. Where the slope is forgiving.
Where rain clouds billow but do not rain.

THE HYPOTHETICAL BAKERY

I have in mind
the pastry shop my great-great-grandfather
Joseph never launched on
Jew Alley before Germany was a country, and
the flat he never built upstairs for
the family he never had, and
the synagogue he never helped grow at the end of
the lane whose name wasn't changed to
Jewel Street in the nineteen twenties when
my grandfather didn't take over, and
the only kosher hotel in town didn't turn to
his gentile rival for strudel,
the grandfather, that is, who never had a J stamped on
his passport nor had his name scrubbed from
the bronze monument to Great War veterans,
and in the end didn't have to sell
the old shop for almost nothing to a certified ethnic, whose
descendants never converted it into
an antique store, and, upon receiving
me decades later, never hesitated to walk me to
the second floor where
my father wasn't born,
having no concern at all that I might see there
a silver bowl, walnut table or fine painting
that had most definitely been in their family for generations, so
they never took great pains to tell me how saddened
their relatives were to see mine sail off to
America, and, in hustling me back to
the station, never went out of their way to avoid
the charred, stained-glass temple windows
that do not now stand as memorial in
the new children's playground right next to the swings, where
the scrolls and the stoves and the sweet rolls
never were.

EVERYTHING

A woman in Frankfurt whisked me
off Taunusstrasse when I was eighteen,
vowing that if I bought her a drink,
we could go directly to her room upstairs
and "do everything."

Though I could only guess
the expanse being offered,
after a shot each of Jägermeister,
when she asked did I want another,
I assured her that no, no,
I was quite ready to retire to her fine apartment
and do everything.

In due course, I bought her Liebfraumilch
and Schnapps, Apfelwein and Löwenbräu
Bellerhof and Bärenfang, soda-water with lime.
I kept paying even after it was clear
I would run out of deutsche marks long before
glimpsing even the suburb of an areola.
Kept paying, giddily at first,
then the way Vegas junketers do,
though in the end I was haunted
by my great aunts and uncles,
behind all that barbed wire,
how they kept on working
and praying.

As I stumbled from Bar Heidi
into the dusk of a world still combing
its anger and shame, I saw that
even though everything
had stepmother eyes and woodcutter hands,
hair the color of Eva Braun's before the bleach,

I had wanted it,
wanted it fondling the buttons of a blouse
rummaged from a corpse, wanted it in a room
with lampshades and ashtrays,
wanted it just for a moment,
but wanted it all.

Squirrel Hill

These heights, these hills, where we've come to rest from fear,
Shaker, Forest, Cherry, Bloomfield, Woodland, Crown,
just rented air; we will not replace you here.

Maybe these ridges will help us disappear,
or see you marching from a neighboring town,
where sight of these hills won't let you rest from fear.

Where we were for years and then we never were,
Pinsk, Trachenbrod, Radzilow, Nizhyn, Savran—
leave the trees bare; we will not replace you here.

What's new about the news is that now it's near.
No, we just forgot that shirt-wise brown is brown,
words do burn, and we can see the rest from here.

We will move on, hope a tricky souvenir.
What then with your native frown, your father's gun?
When we go, our gone will not replace your fear.

Saint Peter, his ample nose, his soured ear—
What if he just has rules, not favorite sons?
Last height, last hill, last hour to own the fear
then get in line; we will not replace you here.

Where Everything Is

was the title of a soft brown leather loose-leaf binder
our father began keeping once he turned seventy-five
and every time thereafter my sister or I visited him

at the Fort Lee co-op he walked us through its chapters
consisting of lists of all physical or documentary items
he called his own and how to find them including

menus of files pouches cartons and their orderly cargo
phone numbers of banks and insurance companies
directional maps to vaults and storage lockers and keys

in plastic packets that led to drawers and fireproof boxes
and other keys and further directions to where more stuff
was hidden in the couch cushions and under the linoleum

he said it was because he had spent so much time
after each of his parents aunts uncles and cousins
had died trying to figure out where their things were

and who was to get what that he didn't want his children
to go through the same on his own passing and for this
we were finally able to begin loving the man who had

beaten us understanding also that when you start with
very little something anything feels like everything which
you must spend your life protecting so you can pass it on

now my sister has the leather binder I have the war albums
and except for a raft of gold coins we left buried shallow
in the closet walls nothing anymore is where it was

Madame Butterfly

She was the kindest woman anyone knew,
though to me the grandma who wanted to talk
when the Yankees were on.
How school was. If I had nice friends.
Her pastille breath, Galore perfume
and mashed potato breasts the organs of suffocation.
Armchair bound by gout with a taut bob of pewter hair,
ringed by jardinières of lilies, she fed me apples
with the tart skin pared off in splendid curls.
Her grasp of the undeniable had saved a family,
moved a stiff-necked man to quit their homeland,
where he was sure reason would return.
But, as she would tell me when we had taken in
yet again the scuffed rendering of her favorite Puccini
and I had remarked on the stupidity
of the heroine's devotion to a jerk,
the story is just housing for the music.
Which I've repeated since to dates in business suits
appalled by Butterfly's sacrifice,
the blade of her voice calling to those
who have lost the trail of love
that you can start again here,
boxed in brilliance,
hanging by a thread.

THE BLUE VIOLINIST

after Marc Chagall (1947)

The Blue Violinist is not blue.
His face is orange, hands white, hair and eyes black,
while just about everything else is blue.
His bench, his socks, the sparrows on his lap,
houses and fences, the night air, even some leaves,
various shades of the same blue.
His world seems to want him also to be blue.
Except for the violin, which is golden.

And the blue baker was not a baker.
Uncle Heinz was a violinist
when only those with the Führer's nose
were authorized to play.
A violinist with knuckles white from flour,
cheeks warmed red,
while the shirts and the trucks were brown.
The bricks and smoke and tongues,
even the edelweiss along the muddy river,
aspects of the same brown.
Except for the shoes,
whose color could not be discerned.

Uncle Heinz baked and baked.
Like his father and father's father.
Baked before he left and on the boat over.
Baked for a new army in the Pacific
and where he settled in the Bronx.
Baked violinist bread.
Violinist rolls, lady fingers, coffee rings and macaroons.
Which came out of the ovens golden.

Chemo and Late Love

Aunt Hilda of the hairy chin mole
that later killed her, and whose father
had been gassed at Treblinka,
leaned over to whisper in my ear
one Thanksgiving when I was eight
that I would never know love
until I saw someone suffer
and wished it were me instead.

I believe I loved Peggy
while our young marriage lasted,
meant to love long-haul flames Jan and Helen,
though none of them suffered much
that I knew of. And I surely loved
my mother at last, clacking dentures,
manic white hair, yet formed no wish
to spell her at the table of pain.

Now the overdue lover, with her all-in ways
her down-and-out blood. So I wish it—
hook me to the eight-hour drip
of four different poisons,
ship me the steroids and antiemetics,
run me to the ER every other week,
buy the mauve yarn and I'll knit the head scarf.

But the code is strict in these parts:
No substitutions, no exchanges.
Only gestures need apply.
I can hold her hand, tell an old joke,
give her a ride.

Hilda, there was so little love in our line
that all I heard you say was suffering.

How's my darling? She worries I'll be sad
without her. And she laughs,
laughs at your linear equation of anguish and heart,
says that when it comes to love,
suffering is not a multiplier, not a diagnostic,
not even a metaphor.

Maybe just a drifter, like you, like me,
looking for a job, for a lateness,
a sweetness, heavy on the vine.

III

Xiu-Xiu

My lover from Texas complains
to me that a Jewish boy in school
keeps telling the daughter
she adopted in China
there is no Santa Claus.

So I tell her girl about the time
I asked my own mom
if we could just once
celebrate Christmas,
then woke to find
tacked to the wall above my bed
an orange inside
one of my father's black socks,

which makes her laugh,
so we say a prayer for mothers,
ours and others,
for the tales born of the deal
their love makes with the world,

how Gretel's goodness needed
not only the hook-nosed hag
and the oven, but also
the mother she never knew,
how the moon required
a raven sky,
and the breadcrumbs
an unbroken light.

Private Sky

If a star is a thousand light-years away,
it has taken the star's light a thousand years
to get here, so the star we are seeing is really
how the star looked a thousand years ago,
not how it looks today.
           —adapted from HowStuffWorks.com

If I were still drinking or a husband,
the Scotch would have found me by now,
keeping company with a loyal porch,
pinholed heaven staring down at no one,
scythe moon risen without a flame of its own.

Instead I'm stretched by the Truckee River,
reading on empty this album of time:
Deneb, giant blue heart of the Swan,
fiercer by thousands than our middle-aged sun,
as it was when Aristotle met the unmoved mover
and Shang Yang first mapped China in his mind.
Rigel, western heel of Orion where the Scorpion stung,
when Saint Francis confessed to his pigeons
and Khan rode the spine of Asia.
Achernar at Gettysburg.
Capella dying yellow to white at the summer of love.
Vega, true north of pre-history,
as it flared on a wedding day.

This once-only whole of distant fires,
not as they are but as they were,
on days sundry and far-flung,
burning in the cold so I can hold them
and be held.

It is a most private sky.

As if on the same dark canvas I could hold
a father prying fingers from the edge of a pool,
a mother's drying breath on the blood from a cut,
a lover frying eggs in another man's kitchen,
the one I should have loved
trying on her gown for a moonless night
when only the stars are out
and there is no borrowed light.

EYEBROWS

When my sister's nine-year-old son,
whose dad has moved to a warmer climate,
asks how he might know if a girl loves him,
I describe the way my ex-wife used to tweeze
the wild as ricegrass ridge
keeping my unfurrowed brow
from each uncertain eye,
plush of her palm cupped beneath my chin,
fingertips grazing my earlobes,
her pupils dutiful, like Penelope's
scanning the glassed horizon.

And her pluck decisive,
one hand doing work, the other taking care,
so I felt the favor in the wound,
took no offense at the thought of improvement
as the dark, the spindly, the wayward
met their match in her noble plan.

My nephew has forgotten his question,
wants only to know if I do my own now.

I tell him don't get used to doing
too much for yourself.

VALERIE

Sometimes after partying at the 2am Club
with her besties from Cleveland and Memphis,
she would slide breathlessly into bed
sweating garlic fries and Cutty Sark.
God, I loved that smell
but would make her wait till first light
for syncopated flying-monkey twister,
or there's a there everywhere mu shu highway,
or bite-the-pillow fifth base and no toys needed.
When I believed we were done,
she would ask what I was thinking.
And I would say "Nothing." Which was true.
So I would ask what she was thinking.
And she would answer "Ninety percent of it
you don't want to know." Which was also true,
since the ten percent included:
a red hoodie, sandpaper and a Viking tattoo;
her va-jay-jay running for mayor of Oakland
and my johnson with its own talk show;
the dream where she lets go
of her son's hand in a railroad crossing.
I didn't just love her.
She was cocaine on the bullet train,
a twerking zombie snowball in Jamaica,
Amy Winehouse on top
in the bathroom of a diving plane.
For all you Nerudas, Gandhis and Houdinis
yet to come: Bring her angry but not dishonest,
stories but not tales, and don't ever believe
you're the one with the guts to be loyal.

The Clone

Though we missed you in different ways,
even in earliest renderings
the body was yours,
down to neckline and navel,
whistle and wink, beryl blue vein.
The first copy didn't know me
but thought she might like to.

So they fused in the facts, the footage—
the girl with a catfish at summer camp,
a rainy bike ride up the coast of Maine.
Those who knew you a bit
from the office, the book club,
were pretty sure, but the weave
was still too loose for specialists,
her impersonations
different enough from yours.

So they added the power
to gather and twine on her own,
by touch and talk, fashion and salvage,
every muted thread,
what no one ever knew.
But she knew what wasn't hers
and that showed through.

So they went to where the singular mind
clings to itself, grieves its own brief time,
flings itself on a heart that isn't flesh,
invents a soul.
Finding there what was ever only yours
they blew it into her
and you rattled in her bed,
some memories lost to sleep,
but feeling yourself,
the free will, the old dreams.

So I asked them to make two more
of me: one as you always wanted—
festive, impetuous, orchids wild but tended;
one as I wanted for you—
less knowing, more curious to be known.

And now you can choose
among the three of us.

ITCH

I can't think right now about the endangered
sage grouse or the new translation of Catullus.
What I need is a mechanical pencil, tip pointed
skyward behind my back, somewhere equivocal
between rhomboid major and latissimus dorsi
along one of the intercostal nerves.

Except the pencil is vertically challenged, can't
reach my wherever from any contorted obliquity.
And the coat hanger is an idiot, or the place
just doesn't exist in the physical world.

Which I would believe to my utter distraction by
spatulas and golf clubs, carrots and doorknobs,
were it not for you, my dear, who can find any
latitude of fugitives or longitude of ghosts,
deep in the dermis or on the corneum's dry bed,
with your unfiled nails, with some blind direction:

Left a little. No, too much. Back the other way.
Sure, we can visit your stepsister in Poland.
Under the tee-shirt please. The longer strokes.
The word comes from Old English and before that
Old Norse (try concentric circles or the symbol
for infinity), so I'm in a long line of sufferers,
from Edward the Confessor to Erik the Red.

Down now. A bit more dig. Almost draw blood.
Yes, right there. Keep going just like that.
Or else it returns. It churns, it chews, it chills,
it chirps imagined brush to brush. It charts your
touch. It chooses when. Scratch me to sleep.
Tomorrow we'll do important things.

The Catch

Night game at Candlestick toward the end of its days.
June Rockwell, season ticket-holder of the so-so Giants,
has lured me out to see the wretched Cubs. First date.
When I pick her up, she asks if I've brought my glove
and I tell her I'm from the Bronx where we do everything
with our bare hands.

Thin crowd, uneventful innings, until two out in the seventh,
when Chicago's lumbering, chaw-spitting right fielder
nicks a rising heater that sails backward several sections
from our box seats into a circular gale like the twister
in *Wizard of Oz*, the ball at its apex still no real concern
twenty rows away.

And yet, in its final moments, the object of common regard
begins to beam intently, inevitably, for my patron's unarmed lap.
I? Bud Light in one hand, fully adorned bratwurst in the other,
no kidding, I refuse to panic, so the hot dog becomes at last
the missing glove, explodes like a grenade as the seamed orb
makes exceptional contact.

When, after a decent interval, I look up, June, standing now,
a Jackson Pollock of ballpark cuisine—tinsels of pork rind and
sauerkraut in her startled hair, glitter of mustard and relish from
brow to chin—says not a word, does not go to wash up, just
lowers her quivering body. The wind dies. The home team fails.
We do not speak on the drive back.

Ah, what might have been. But not for me. I'm romantic in that
other way. This way. For this night, no if-only will ever rival what
happened. Watch as we reach June's flat, she turns, caked still
with the spectacle I have made of gallantry and kisses me.
Softly, briefly, decisively. Watch the fog rise to claim her
for the perfect past.

On Being Slapped By a Woman I Don't Know

Intermission at the Opera. Saturday night.
All I know about her is the pageboy cut
of raven red hair. She stands abruptly
then uses the full arc of her body turn
to imprint the left side of my face.
One contact lens now lodged up under its eyelid,
a bicuspid stuck to the inside of my mouth,
my cheek like a pup tent smacked by lightning.
I had never been slapped by a woman before,
though there was something about it I missed.
Bacall giving it to Bogie. Crawford to Gable.
Deserved. Delivered. On to the next scene.
Black and white. Mine seemed technicolor.
Turns out, she had been twirling one tip
of her reading glasses between her front teeth
while the other tip was tickling her ear.
Which she thought was me, from the row behind,
flirting, or trying to filch one of her diamond studs.
Probably some other guy had earned it.
Or I had earned it elsewhere.
Edging my hand under Faye Brown's iron bra,
her dad glued to *Gunsmoke* downstairs.
Teasing my ex-wife for airballing a foul shot
in front of 20,000 fans during halftime
at the Oakland Coliseum on taco night.
Asking my mom, just before heading off to college,
why she let her kids be whipped
and what she got out of watching.
I was a good boy once.
May have been an okay man.
Though the heart never believes this.
Needs a sharp reset. A briskly wiped slate.
That's what I missed. The clarity.

And the wakeup doesn't hurt much,
requires no response.
Just blink a few times, wiggle the jaw.
Welcome rough justice.
The curtain is rising.
Carmen is taking her mark.

THE COLONOSCOPAI

There ought to be a Greek name for the ex-lovers who
(because the clinic won't let you drive yourself or take a cab)
come pick you up and take you home from the outpatient
procedure where you were drugged to disremember
what went on with that sleek, fiber-optic tube.

More specifically, in my case: Christine, when I was 51,
whose bulimic daughter had drowned herself in the jacuzzi;
at 58, Lee, public defender whose pederast client
was out shopping again in the Oakland Walmart;
at 63, Maria, who had just learned her uncle was her father.

I wasn't supposed to be single at those ages, but
a wife could not have kept it so simple, would have
had questions, taken care of me in unwanted ways,
not understood there is an art to forgetting.

And these women, long consigned to the list of friends
I rarely saw, answered the call without asking,
drove the two miles quietly, past the Shell, the Save Mart
the park carousel, giving me time to fill my mind again
with a campout in Haleakala crater, silverswords and
the eyes of old pack mules glazed by the Milky Way,
with Hula Hoops naked, leading to reverse cowgirl
in a rocking chair on a rotten porch in Chico,
with Mahler's 6th two days after 9/11, the cellists in tears.

The closest might be Mnemosyne, goddess of recall,
who slept with Zeus for nine straight nights (not
because he was nice, but because he had experience),
then bore the Muses, who knew instinctively the need,
in their work, for memory; not so much of what happened
but to replace what happened with what can be told—
field song sung to the freeborn grandkids,
volta scratched on a bedpost, woolly mammoth brushed
in its own bright blood on the walls of a Spanish cave.

TEA

We went to London once a year and,
aside from conjugate acts in challenging places,
there was one thing she loved doing
in that conurbation only, made personal
by her novel use of accouterments
(strainer, drip tray, sugar tongs, cozy)
and especially how the milk was introduced—
smallest possible liquid dollop
that pricked the fuscous pond,
dove for a skipped heartbeat,
then resurfaced in one of three avatars:
mushroom cloud,
gossamer of cracked glass or,
to her repulsed fascination,
simply itself, the unaltered bolus.
Questioning would be like asking Magritte
what's with the derby, or how come the apple
and why green.
Actually, someone did ask him. He said
everything we see hides another thing
and we always want to see what's hidden.

THE SCIENTIST

Ponce was on to something. The magic of youth.
Though South Florida, it turns out, not the place to search.

My love, whom the world needs more than it needs me,
needs a bone marrow transplant—the collection of stem cells
from her blood for re-introduction after extreme chemo.
They are looking for the youngest cells, the uncorrupted.

But on Tuesday, her count of these, per the hemocytometer,
is six, too low to even start the process. Twenty-five,
they say, is the goal, forty would be fabulous.
They will search again Wednesday.
A Filipino nurse named Teo tells her as she leaves
that the young cells will come out of hiding
if someone rubs the arches of her feet.

Which someone will be me that evening,
after I research the concept like the scientist I am,
discovering it to be ridiculous even by Internet standards,
where endorsed stimulants include sweet potatoes
and weightlifting, but nothing remotely podiatric. Still,
I do like her feet. Midwestern. Optimistic. True.

We start out a bit confused. Did he mean rub or massage?
Top, side or bottom? I show her a plastic card,
correlating regions of the sole to internal organs,
that a coed-turned-shaman gave me in the 60s,
after we shared an interesting night.
My love is not convinced,
though while pressing and squeezing for a full forty minutes,
I can't resist some attention to the base of her pinky toes,
which apparently commune with her earlobes.
She asks if chatting would break my concentration.

Wednesday morning, the only number that means something
isn't the Dow or how many runs the Giants scored.
It's seventy-nine.

Who knew that at my age I could do anything
to interest the young. Who knew how ready I had become
to abandon science and play the goddamn Pied Piper.
I see all those bright cells texting each other as they leave
the comfort of the marrow for what my fingers have promised
will be the role of their lives.

TRUXEL ROAD

for the women of California

Just another white on pine-green name
for no place, those hundred-odd drives
back from Tahoe to the Bay,
till we turned there a week into August
where Routes 5 and 80
cross the heart of a dreamed-up state.

Pam's third-grade boy had dumped a bonsai
on her mom's pearl rug in Truckee,
flipped heirloom photos face-down in the john,
peed on drapes, torn through lawn chairs,
barfed up pie in the pool. No one home there
next morning when we dropped by for breakfast
and the boy still kicking in his car seat two hours west
where we quit just not to kill something
at the great washboard arch vowing help for all strays:
Rite Aid and Safeway, Pep Boys and Sleep Train…
though Pam just took cider from the shack girl
with a shiner and snake sleeve tattoo,
then smiled toward wind-gashed hills
where her grandma's great grandma once spat chaw
on the dust of a late husband's claim.

X marks the spot where the women we want
have a love we can't follow,
where the souls of Califia's tanned hell-cats
still hunt boar with gold-tipped spears,
where Luza Wilson once banked flakes
in her mattress and oven
for miners who had muled fifty miles
just to glance at her sun-bleached hair.

IV

OTTER

Steward of a breakwater kelp state
and its thicket of parenthetical subjects
(orange garibaldi, bluish blacksmith,
señorita fish like a yellow cigar,
bat star and puffball sponge,
gumboot chiton, cabezon,
turban snail and dragon eel),

he swims for miles like a rubber torpedo
from Pigeon Point to Morro Bay,
claims his fill of escargot and calamari
leaving only morsels for the gulls. But
they also make him eat a ton of urchins
so his teeth turn purple by the time he's three.
Once in a while, he gets to drift on his back
cracking an oyster against his belly with a rock.

He's for when you turn fifty single,
cashing a paycheck just ahead of the rent,
well past the days of horses and lions,
not yet ready for the company of birds.

Thick-necked, flat-eared and side-eyed,
back East he'd be playing rugby
or whistling for a rush hour cab.
Out here his friends wrap him in seaweed
so he can rest. Rest
from endlessly burping his oily coat
to ward off frost, rest
from mating unpleasantly, rest
from sniffing the breeze with a tilted snout
for the guns of traders
long gone from these waters.

APES FOR PANDAS

A few years after Nixon forged the deal with China
that brought Ling-Ling and Hsing-Hsing to Washington,
in the period of our history known as Panda Diplomacy,
I was assigned to represent the San Francisco Zoo,
which had recently built a natural habitat
for Western Lowland Gorillas.
The mayor at the time, anxious to approach the Chinese
with the idea of trading a few of our apes
for some of their pandas,
asked me to craft a Great Ape–Panda Exchange Agreement
for which, as you might imagine, there was no template.
So I drove to the intersection of Sloat Boulevard
and the Great Highway to check out the currency.
Particularly Bwanda, the patriarch, born in the rain forests
of Cameroon, black and shiny as the hood of a Mercedes,
except for a silver swath on his back and a russet crown.
He had a taste for grass, and slept at the foot
of an obeche tree, his family on the branches above.
One of his daughters, Koko, became world-famous
for learning a thousand English words in sign language,
then asking for two kittens at Christmas,
whom she named Lipstick and Smokey. But that was later.
Although the mayor envisioned twin 747s landing
simultaneously at SFO and Shanghai International,
my draft of the Agreement called for a Cold War-style swap
across a bridge on an unnamed volcanic atoll in the Pacific,
as if the exchangees were decorated military brass.
The mayor met me with a look that said *you are not my friend*,
so I spoke of the indignity of trading our nearest relatives
for pea-brained furballs the world had fallen in love with
because they resembled a six-year-old's stuffed pillow.
I was removed from the project.
                    In the dream, I walk Bwanda and three of his kin
to the midpoint of the bridge, where we meet the pandas.

The alpha panda growls and Bwanda pretends to be impressed,
nods to the mammalian king of a different continent,
rises, and roars. The bridge rattles.
He moves on, turning back briefly with deep-set eyes
from a day ten million years ago
when his forebears and ours went their separate ways.

LAND'S END

As the light comes up, first shorebirds come in
one by one to tip the steepled granite
where surf breaks black to blue to white,
then their kin fill in quietly below
as a stream's bustle spills the tide sideways and slips
a bleached herring bone from its windowpane stone.
Plumes of gold bottle grass never enlighten
the igneous char and tilted slate,
nor do cormorants believe in the squall,
gravid kelp swales or sardines shivered down,
just as lizard and rock have different knowledge
of each other, yesterday, the gutted cliffs, the sun.
You may find you aren't needed, which is not the same
as unwelcome, and there is an order without design.

THE PATH OF TOTALITY

Our entire business park has massed at the fountain
mid-morning to watch the Great American Eclipse
trace its calculated arc from Salem to Sumter.
This used to be Ra or Yahweh shouting Behold! Beware!
Now those whiz kids from the office next door, on break
from inventing how to store the brain outside the body,
are heard to whisper "I could do that,"
as a cell phone tower darkens to the west.
One of our two main celestial bodies, precisely
400 times smaller, but also precisely 400 times closer,
is moving to perfectly cover the other.
We will turn our backs in a modern syzygy
of selfie-self-earth-moon-sun,
adding to what is in shadow.
That which has become coincidence
does not return to miracle.
Though we still want the feeling.
Of mystery, of augury, of being warned.
The feeling that this all bends toward wholeness.
This need of the spare, cold minion with a dark side
to blot the only light by which it is seen.
This need of the master to show a blistering crown.
Which we could see just this once without going blind,
were we looking rather than capturing,
were we not already remembering.
Smile. Two thumbs up. Click.
We were here.
The stars are out at noon.

UNIDENTIFIED OBJECTS

Blow off that tee time
and head to the Ninth Annual UFO Expo
at the San Jose DoubleTree,
featuring a keynote by the ex-Governor of Utah—
who knows what he saw.

Conference veterans, munching hot dogs and sushi
as if shape-shifting were simply bourgeois,
will swear your parents are imposters
and most of history is not our fault.

You can take in talks about panspermia,
or secret government mining operations on the moon;
a workshop on surgery to remove alien implants
by the professor who wrote the *Star Trek Cookbook*,
or another on Pleiadian procedures
for healing the force field between the sexes
to which it's suggested you bring a large towel;
or a video about the odyssey of one Fred Reagan—
his Cessna was winged by beings
resembling metallic asparagus who,
as redress, shrunk his prostate.

So it all sounds encouraging.
Anyway, your buddies have filled out
the usual foursome with a refreshing stranger
who finds a lost Titleist in the thirteenth fairway,
looks around to make sure no one's watching,
then gives the orb a moonstruck whack
toward a distant hotel rooftop where
with the zoom on your cell phone camera
you snap it spinning oblong
just above the trees.

GOD'S WIDOW

His son wasn't hers and the spirit never as holy
as biographers made out. Halfway through
the sixth day she told him he looked tired, said
nothing's wrong with free will, but coupling it
with the directive to have dominion could take
a bad turn; instead give more power to the whales
or trees, or the moon. But no. Then all those nights
in the basement working on his special project.

Not mother or minder, Thelma, Heloise, or the Virgin
Queen. She is the Other. Capital Oh. And now
I have to pray to her. She whose love was not
enough, whose dear I was never, whose green home
has been savaged, who couldn't care less if I believe.
My girlfriend says I might want to start on my knees.

WELLS FARGO

Hunched right behind me in Kafka's bank line,
an octogenarian with 49ers cap askew
and white stubble as old as his last floss,
grunts, *Slowest in the Western States,*
so I ask him how he knows,
and he snorts, *Don't be a smart-ass,*
informs me he's hiding from the social director
of his assisted living center, volunteers
some inside scoop on the distant tellers:
One only does wire transfers to South America;
the other isn't yet trained to handle cash.
A supervisor with the name tag "Jerry"
is cruising the crowd ready to apologize
in English, Spanish or Tagalog
for whatever no one else is sorry about.
The old dude tells him he's feeling
estranged from his capital, says,
All I need are a couple of crisp hundreds
to give as Christmas tips to my barber
and my life coach. Jerry offers him a Dum-Dum
and some hand sanitizer with aloe. I offer
to get him scratch paper so he can write a poem.
He mumbles:
Roses are black,
my nose just bled,
and my balls itch,
so I'm not dead.
Then he asks if we can switch places—
Time is running out faster for me, he says.
At which point I have to question
whether any of this actually happened,
or if it's just a talk I'm having with myself
twenty years from now,
in line for something else I think is mine,
or I want to buy,
or I've already paid for.

Milpitas Sunset

Fifty miles south of where lovers with maps
are snapping backlit photos of a bridge,
crooked street, square named for chocolate
and town hall dipped in gold,
most folks have an immigrant heart.
They never dream of going back
or of staying here either,
where the sun's brass
is just the end of another day's work,
pilot light for a saucepan
in which neon arrows blink on and on
through the musk of charbroiled burgers.
Where the chatter of Bangalore and Manila
floods the deck of the Banana Lounge,
and the bones of bronze-skinned farmers
who once sold flax at this old truck stop
between Oakland and San Jose
clatter under shrinking cornfields.
Where those who haven't been here too long
squint past slack wires and salt pond haze
at a blank orange canvas spreading west.

CARAVANSARY

My buddy asks why they call it *independent living*,
then answers his own question: "Because it's not."

About a hundred geriatric women and seven men
are figuratively connected by yards of yellowed
plastic tubing propagating from hissing oxygen tanks
like a root system they dragged with them from
the old country to yet another barren passage.

A man from Oaxaca trims hedges in two feet of snow.
Half-solved jigsaws splay in dust on card tables.
Tootsie's in the social hall for the fifth time this month.
A Matagalpan woman slips a brownie into a widow's
beaded purse. Sittercise, story time, something hurts
every day, and there's no bazaar at the end of this slog,
though two grizzled girlfriends parade the latest walkers
as if shopping underwater, for what they cannot say.

A mason from Mixco helps a grandma from Yonkers
make solitaire moves on a rococo tray in her bed.
A teacher from Soyapango sets place cards for dinner.
No salt allowed, nothing to die for, so suicides
are beside the point and elevator talk quite civil,
even by those who were vile for their first eighty years.
Sons do stop by, with their sons, for the family day buffet.

Sovereignty and asylum in the eye of the beholder,
here is the junction of two endless goings,
the ego's laundromat, where rashes spread like wildfires
but nothing is more contagious than dignity,
much of which radiates from kitchen and garden:
Their names are Rosa, Beatriz, Miguel and Hernán.

So it's OK not to give a fuck what papers they have
and just thank them for looking after our mothers.

AT MILE ROCKS

From Point Lobos, named by the Spanish
for barking seals they decided were wolves,
you can see near the breakers,
on a black lava outcrop barely above the swell,
a column, twenty feet high,
red and white stripes almost faded to bone.

Some say it's the stump of a sea-swept lighthouse
built, after a steamer from Rio went down in the fog,
not by engineers, who refused, but by seamen,
their wives still roaming Land's End with flashlights,
only the base intact now,
a salt lick for pigeons and gulls.

Some say it's the work of immigrant Wu Zhao
who raised a pillar at the mouth of the Bay,
then boated out daily for months
to etch the names of forced laborers
into her squat limestone creation, until,
while carving out the character for "slave,"
she slipped and let go.

It's a nice hike over to the crusted beach
closest to Mile Rocks, along failing cliffs,
the Golden Gate Bridge at your back.
Among maze walkers and unleashed poodles,
backpackers and stockbrokers
rinsing toes in the surf, you may meet
a spent mariner staring out to sea
or share the shoreline with a woman from Kunming
who's been out to mix with ghosts,
laid joss sticks and tossed blossoms.

And you may wonder why both stories
can't be true. Why the dead
to whom sailor and stranger are paying respects
aren't your dead too.

Borrowed Light

The morning star here
has to inch its way
up the scruffs of mountains,
so its sway is as thin as the air
long after first light.

Misreading at times through an eyelid
the charged tonics of dawn,
there are nights you rise fooled
to keep company instead
with the humpbacked moon,
its sunlit dial and tethered rounds.

Since all the pocked rock has
is offered up,
your heart tells you to say
this is everything you need,
though it is not warmth, not bread, not love.

So you borrow what has been borrowed
to disquiet the hours and ways
that go out darkly from here,
and you stitch a quilt of strange comfort
from the debt of this light,
where Washoe ghosts
truck with Donner bones
and the stricken tongues of wolves.

SPEAKING IN TONGUES

My lover sometimes sits up at 2 a.m.
like a jackknife and says something like,
"I put the couch in the microwave,"
though more often she just offers a string
of impenetrable syllables, then re-engages
her pillow and the peace of the unsaid.
Which takes me back to Freshman year
when a young woman stood suddenly
midway through a lecture on Plato's Cave,
spoke gibberish for three minutes straight,
then stopped just as abruptly, and said
to the class, "I don't know why God has chosen
to speak through me today, but He loves you."
Of course, I imagined sleeping with her,
the Cher-haired messenger in a peasant dress,
not because I wanted the translation,
because I wanted the transport—
to be that possessed, that called.
At the dawn of my seduction by language,
I knew that its mind was not enough.
I needed someone to speak for its body,
its suet and thew, its love affair with the tongue
unvexed by meaning or context.
I needed the vocables
our hirsute ancestors used before knowing
to what or whom they might wake,
the words whose work is not to tell us
but to reach us, dream to dream
in the middle of the night.

ACKNOWLEDGMENTS

Special thanks to my extraordinary teachers, Sharon Olds, Joe Millar, Dorianne Laux, Ellen Bass, and Brenda Hillman; if there is craft, intellect, heart or courage in these pages, this is significantly due to their outsized generosity of time and spirit. Appreciation also to my posse of fellow travelers, Amanda Moore, Barb Reynolds, Devika Brandt, Janet Jennings, Pat Zylius, and Stewart Mintzer—they were always the first to suffer, providing hope and direction nonetheless. A shout out to Joe Millar, Kwame Dawes and Susan Gardner for helping organize and edit this book. A big hug for Kathy Evans and Sally Doyle, who teach the weekly poetry workshop that I have been lucky to sponsor for a decade at UCSF Benioff Children's Hospital, as well as for all the inspiring young people who have graced its hallowed rooms. And gratitude beyond words to Susan Bonetto, my compass, my shelter, my magic, my love.